How to love till the end:
A manual for unrelenting love

Emily S. Alvarado

Table of contents

CHAPTER 1

Love is an all-encompassing concept that includes a wide variety of powerful and positive mental and emotional states, ranging from the highest form of virtue or a good habit to the most profound form of interpersonal attachment and down to the purest form of pleasure. The love of a mother is distinct from the love of a spouse, which is distinct from the love for food. This range of meanings is illustrated by the fact that the love of a mother is distinct from the love of a spouse. Love is most frequently understood to relate to a sensation that combines intense desire with a sense of emotional commitment.

Love is viewed as having both positive and negative aspects, with its virtue equating to human kindness, compassion, and affection, as "the unselfish loyal and benevolent concern for the good of another," and its vice equating to human moral flaws such as vanity, selfishness, amour-propre, and egotism, as having the potential to lead people into mania, obsessiveness, or codependency. Love is viewed as having both positive and negative Acts of compassion and love may also be directed toward oneself, other people, or animals and fall under this category. Because of its fundamental significance to a person's psyche, love, in all of its incarnations, is one of the most frequently explored topics in the creative arts. It also plays an important role in the development of interpersonal relationships. It has been hypothesized that love serves the purpose of keeping human beings together in the face of threats and ensuring the survival of the species as a whole.

Over the last two decades, there has been a substantial expansion in the study of emotion in the scientific community. According to the color wheel theory of love, there are a total of twelve different types of romantic relationships, which are broken down as follows: three main, three secondary, and nine tertiary. According to the triangle theory of love, the three pillars of a healthy love relationship are "intimacy, passion, and commitment." Love may also be understood in a religious or spiritual context. In comparison to other emotional states, it is much more challenging to provide a definition that adequately captures the essence of love due to the wide variety of contexts in which it may be used and the complexities of the sensations it evokes.

The concept of "love" may refer to several interconnected but separate ideas depending on the setting in which it is used. Many other languages have more than one word to represent some of the many notions that are referred to as "love" in English; one example of this is the variety of meanings that the word "love" may have in Greek (agape, eros, philia, and storge). The formulation of a universal definition is made extra difficult by the fact that different cultures have different ways of conceiving what love is.

Although the nature or substance of love is a matter of constant controversy, distinct parts of the word may be defined by establishing what isn't love (antonyms of "love") (antonyms of "love"). Hatred is often used as a contrast to love, which can be thought of as a more robust form of like. Love is an expression of positive sentiment in general (or neutral apathy). Love, on the other hand, is seen as a sort of romantic connection that is less sexual and more emotionally intimate than its counterpart, desire. Even though the term "love" is often used to refer to close friendships or platonic affection, love is sometimes defined as an interpersonal connection that has romantic connotations and is sometimes contrasted with friendship. (Further probable misunderstandings emerge with usages "girlfriend", "boyfriend", and "simply close buddies").

Love, when addressed in a general sense, often refers to a sensation that one person has for another person. Love often entails a person or thing—including oneself—being cared for or identified by the person or object loving (cf. the vulnerability and care theory of love) (cf. narcissism). In addition to variances in how love is understood amongst different cultures, views about love have also undergone significant evolution throughout history. Even though evidence of romantic ties may be found as far back as ancient times in the form of love poetry, some historians place the origin of contemporary concepts of romantic love in courtly Europe during or during the Middle Ages.

The intricate and abstract character of love sometimes turns speech about love into a thought-terminating cliché. Love is the subject of several well-known proverbs, including Virgil's "Love conquers everything" and "All You Need Is Love" by The Beatles. In line with Aristotle's definition of love, Saint Thomas Aquinas describes it as "the wish to do well for another." Love, according to Bertrand Russell, is a condition of "absolute value," as opposed to relative value. [Citation needed] [source: missing citation] Philosopher Gottfried Leibniz argued that love is "to be thrilled by the pleasure of another." According to Meher Baba, one of the characteristics of love is an "active recognition of the inherent value of the object of love," as well as a "sense of togetherness." The term "unconditional selflessness" is how Jeremy Griffith, a biologist, characterizes love.

CHAPTER 2

These 14 Steps Will Make Your Love Last Forever

It's one thing to find someone you love, but it's a whole other challenge to keep that love alive for a lifetime. We all want a relationship that will last, but how do we find it? This is the other question that is asked frequently, and there is no one correct response to it. People ask it in addition to wondering how they can make money. You have to understand that the act of falling in love is only the beginning of the process; the true challenge lies in maintaining the love that has been won. Don't believe anyone who tries to convince you otherwise; love is hard work. This may be the greatest type of job there is, but there's no getting past the fact that it's still labor.

Following what seemed like an endless courtship, one of my friends finally broke up with the person she loved. Then, she started dating the man who would later become her husband. She was uncertain, damaged, and uneasy about herself. "With his actions and his understanding, he slowly but surely showed me what genuine love is like," she said. After that, when he made his proposal and we were married, I pledged myself that I would do all in my power to ensure that this marriage would be successful. "It's taken a lot of effort, and there have been highs and lows along the way, but it's been 25 years now, and I'm certain that I now know how to make a relationship last a lifetime," she added.

When it comes to romantic relationships, it is often believed that "forever" is an illusion. But if you ask

people who have been in a relationship for a very long time and are still very much in love with each other, they will tell you that love changes from being euphoric to being mundane with time, but that if you continue to work on it, you can make a relationship last forever.

So, what is the secret to making love last forever? If you put these 14 suggestions into practice, you can ensure that the love you have for your partner will never fade.

1. Develop confidence within a partnership.

The building of trust in a relationship is an ongoing process. When uncertainty enters our minds, we tend to be extremely critical of ourselves and most other people. However, we need to keep in mind that uncertainty is just another form of fear, and fear is an instinct that is designed to forewarn us and keep us safe. It is imperative that we take the warning seriously, show respect for it, and not allow it to control the relationship.

It takes patience and a willingness to be vulnerable to trust someone, but love requires that you do so to go ahead. If you want your love to last for all of the time, you must have trust for one another and must never let even the tiniest amount of uncertainty enter the picture.

2. Physical closeness is holy

In virtually all romantic partnerships, achieving a comfortable level of physical closeness is a fundamental need. Unless you are asexual, in which case you may skip this paragraph and go on to the next one

(No condemnation, everyone is free to love). Compatibility between two bellies, or "belly to belly" compatibility as I like to refer to it, may sometimes take time but is something worth investing in.

No of the ages of the persons in a relationship, having satisfying sexual encounters is an important means of communicating. It maintains the vitality of the partnership. If you want your relationship to endure a lifetime, you need to continue to work on being more physically intimate with one another.

3. **Respect must be cultivated if you want your relationship to endure a lifetime.**

This is the foundation upon which a love that lasts a lifetime is built. Integrity cannot exist in a

relationship if there is no mutual respect. It is possible that you and the other person do not have the same politics, morals, or ideals; nonetheless, if you do not respect the other person, there will be no equilibrium in the relationship, and it will wither and die. If you love someone, respecting them requires treating them in a manner that will make them feel good about themselves, and this requires supporting the decisions they make. Even if you believe it is for your benefit, being subjected to constant criticism may have a detrimental effect on you. Your manner of interaction with the one you love—including your words, your deeds, and everything else about it—must be laced with respect at all times.

4. Sincerity is the engine that makes everything go.

In case you can't believe it, you don't always have to tell the truth when you're in a committed relationship. Figuring out when to tell a fib is essential. When I say this, of course, I'm referring to little white lies. You have a winning situation when you are aware that your spouse does not look their best but you nevertheless tell them that they are killing it. It's possible that you are not being honest or speaking the truth, but as long as it's not doing any damage, it's not a problem.

The world of love would come to a halt without little white lies, and every relationship needs them to function properly. It's okay to tell some white lies. Every couple does such things, but if you want your relationship to

survive a lifetime, you should make sure that you never lie to each other in a manner that might be damaging. That is horrible for a relationship.

5. **Have the same objectives.**

The concept of falling in love for the sake of having children is so out of style at this point that we don't even want to bring it up. Even while individuals keep having children, we can no longer consider this to be the primary motivation for love. Then, what is the primary cause behind this? Communal objectives People have the desire to construct empires together. No matter whether it's a company, a belief system, or something else. The modern couple does not necessarily aspire to have a large, traditional Indian family.

Having a shared value system is essential if you want your relationship to survive a lifetime.

The majority of individuals need a shared or at least comparable set of values to be able to create empires and work for a common objective. You see, it's not about loving someone who has wonderful values; if you have values that are "lower or higher" than they have in your view, the relationship is going to be unbalanced and unhealthy for both parties. If, on the other hand, you and your significant other have a value system that is compatible with one another, then you are in the ideal situation in which you do not need to worry about or speculate on whether or not they will approve of you on the level of values.

This is the quality that distinguishes good partners, whether in romantic or platonic relationships. If you and your partner don't mind shifting the cash about to escape taxes or if you and your partner would instantly terminate the employee for using sexist language in the workplace, it doesn't matter whether other people think your shared values are questionable or not. They have to be criteria that both of you take into consideration.

6. Allow each other some room

A healthy break from each other, whether it be once a day or once a month, is necessary to keep that love growing. It is important to make time for yourself. Not only does distance make the heart grow fonder, but it also allows you to organize and clear out your mental closet, which ensures

that you do not have any suppressed feelings that surface out of nowhere and surprise you in the future.

In a romantic partnership, having some personal space is not only not a negative thing but is necessary. Give each other some space if you want your relationship to endure a lifetime together.

7. Allow one another to develop.

It takes two individuals to have a romantic connection, and although it is an essential component of a person, it is not the only thing that makes up a person. If a person's romantic partnership comes to dominate everything else in their life, it will eventually start to stifle and suffocate them. This will happen if the relationship becomes the defining aspect of their existence. Therefore, it is equally crucial to focus on who you are aside from your romantic relationships. It is what enables you to love the other person as a distinct and independent being in their own right.

The song "Losing Your Identity in Love" made famous by Arijit Singh may have a romantic ring to it, but in fact, doing so causes more problems than it solves. If you want your love to last a lifetime, you will need to encourage and support one another's personal development. This is the only way for the two of you to flourish together as a couple.

8. Comprehend one another's requirements.

All your partner may want is for you to make him or her a cup of coffee in the morning. Keep a smile on your face when you serve them. It's a significant deal when you think about it, the delight you get from doing something kind for another person.

It may be necessary for you to get together with your man friends once a week. If she ensures that you can do it and never has any qualms about you walking in a bit late and a bit tipsy every Friday night, then it is a wonderful feeling to know that your life partner understands what makes you happy. If she ensures that you can do it, and if she never has any qualms about you walking in a bit late and a bit tipsy every Friday night, then she

9. **Having no trouble expressing gratitude or contrition**

Some individuals believe that expressing "thank you" between two spouses is an overly formal way to express gratitude. To be honest, no. Simply expressing gratitude may go a long way toward ensuring the longevity of a relationship. As soon as you begin to use the phrase "thank you," you become aware of the power that "thank you" has to improve the quality of your connection.

In a similar vein, apologizing to your spouse should be something that just naturally occurs to you. You should never give apologizing for a second thought before doing so.

10. Be forgiving

People who have been successful in making their love last forever will tell

you that the capacity and readiness to forgive one another is the most important trait in a romantic connection.

Mistakes are part of the human experience; nonetheless, it is not wise to dwell on past transgressions or to bring them up in every argument. Your connection will suffer as a direct result of this. Some married couples can recover their trust after one partner has committed adultery, and even endure the experience of having their partner cheat.

11. Reminiscing about times gone by

You are going to learn a lot about love. When couples get together, they are usually excited to chat about how they met. The story of how they first met, when they decided to be married,

and every other minute detail. They would tell their children and even their grandkids these heartwarming tales of love and friendship as they were growing up.

If you want to have a relationship that lasts a lifetime with someone, you should speak about the little things about it that make you tick and that keep the spark of love alive even after many years of marriage.

12. Frequent kissing

This does not need much work on either of your parts, but it is a simple demonstration of how much you care for each other via an act of intimacy. Things like giving your significant other a kiss goodbye before you leave the house and doing the same thing when you see one other again in the

evening are things that keep a relationship alive.

Stealing kisses from one another while you are watching a romantic movie or scene is a terrific technique to ensure that love will stay forever in your relationship. This has absolutely nothing to do with your ages; rather, it reveals how you feel about each other as a couple.

13. **Have your jokes that no one else knows.**

It is beneficial to the longevity of a relationship for both parties to have a healthy sense of humor. And the success of a relationship may be directly attributed to the inside jokes, the playful teasing, and the general good time that both parties enjoy with one another.

If you ask any couple that has been together for a significant amount of time about their inside jokes, you can be sure that they will produce a large quantity of them. Also, some couples have the cutest nicknames for one another, which may evolve over time, but these adorable names have something in them that may make a relationship continue for the rest of one's life.

14. Prepare yourself for an exciting experience.

When a couple is committed to one another for the long haul, the relationship might get tedious. Therefore, if you want to keep the zing alive, you should go on some adventures as often as possible, both little and large.

You have just learned of a new and inviting eatery that is located on the other side of town, and you are prepared to take both the train and the bus to get there. It's like a little mini-adventure to locate that one spot with your significant other that you just adore. Then why not combine your snorkeling adventure with a scuba diving excursion on your next vacation? Alternatively, you may spend your whole life preparing for that experience in a hot-air balloon. There are instances when just having a conversation about the things you both like doing might help your relationship succeed.

CHAPTER 3

Love languages

It seems that there is no universally applicable recipe for love. Who could have predicted that? There is a good chance that the solution is not a one-size-fits-all recipe either. However, the five love languages do provide an intriguing concept and several basic suggestions, tactics, and hints that might assist you in laying out your wants and wishes after you have determined which language speaks to you the most. It should come as no surprise that we all give and receive love in our unique ways, nor should it come as a surprise that your relationship or partners may not necessarily share your philosophical orientation. These "love languages" can help us bridge those gaps and teach us how to identify and ask for what we want and need in life. They

can also help us learn how to love ourselves better.

The following list of love languages might be beneficial to your connection.

1. **Affirming Words and Phrases**

Words of affirmation may take many forms—from simply saying "I love you" to expressing gratitude to another person for their efforts—but their overall effect is to make us feel more valued, welcomed, and loved. Words may be a very significant component of communication for some individuals, as well as a window into their sense of self-worth. People's self-esteem may be improved by positive or negative usage of language.
The best way to offer is to be generous with words of encouragement

whenever someone you care about requires them. Even a simple expression of gratitude, such as "thank you for making supper" or "you look lovely," may do wonders for someone's spirit. Make use of your words so that they might provide delight.
How to Receive: When someone compliments you, you shouldn't discount it, deflect it, or immediately reciprocate. You should also avoid discounting the compliment. Take your time to process it, and savor it.

2. Service-Related Activities

When it comes to some individuals, it is significant if another person does something pleasant for them. The smallest gestures of kindness, such as offering to walk someone else's dog when you see that they already have their hands full or purchasing

someone a bottle of wine to have to wait for them when they come home after a long day, may go a very long way. People might feel more noticed when acts of service are performed for them.
Donating: Here's How: Even though they demand a tiny amount of thinking and space, gentle small acts of service for someone assist both emotionally and physically. Take a burden off, figure out what needs to be done, and get it done, or ask your spouse what you can do to assist them and see what they suggest. The challenge is to carry out these deeds without harboring resentment against anybody.
When someone is doing acts of service for you, the proper way to receive them is to do so with grace. Negating how something is being done is the single most effective way

to halt an act of service dead in its tracks.

3. Gift Getting

Small tokens of affection have long been connected with the act of gift-giving. This is another one of the love languages that has been associated with the misconception that a person yearns for material possessions, but the truth is a little bit more nuanced than that. These presents may be concrete means for someone to be reminded that they are loved and cherished, and rather than being seen as a trivial gesture, they need to be interpreted as something more profound.
The act of presenting a gift does not need any extensive preparation or ceremony. This is not a discussion

about flashy vehicles and dazzling tiaras. Even something as simple as choosing a flower when you're out for a stroll or purchasing a tiny chocolate bar on the way back from the shop might serve as a gentle reminder to the recipient that you were indeed thinking of them throughout that time.

The proper way to accept anything is to show gratitude even for the smallest of gestures and to go beyond the superficial aspects of the situation to get to the core of the issue. If you can tap into the satisfaction that comes from helping others, then the situation will turn into a wonderful win for all parties involved.

4. Spending time together

Some married couples make a big deal out of having quality time together, and for good reason. Giving

your spouse your complete and undivided attention for at least some of the time you spend together helps to establish a deeper connection, makes individuals feel appreciated and heard, and facilitates the creation of a shared life for the two of you.
Donating: Here's How: When we speak about spending quality time together, what we mean is that we won't try to multitask. Instead of pretending to listen or just tuning out, try actively participating in the conversation by turning off the phone and the television.
The Way to Take in: Recognize that although spending time together is important for some people, individuals also need their own space and that it is enormously useful for a healthy and balanced relationship to not do everything together or spend every waking hour together.

5. Touching Someone's Body

The focus of closeness, touch, and physical contact does not always have to be sexual all of the time. Hugs and other physical displays of affection may be a cause of discomfort for some individuals, yet for others, even the smallest expressions of closeness can mean the world. If you or your partner craves that physical touch, then asking for it can be essential for you to feel loved, recognized, desired, and stable in your relationship. If you or your partner craves that physical touch, then ask for it.
Donating: Here's How: It is not always necessary to make really large demonstrations; instead, it is sufficient to just embrace someone, touch them on the shoulder, or hold their hand. If this is tough for you, try not to be hesitant in communicating

this to your spouse and addressing the reasons why so that they do not get the impression that it is all about them.

The Way to Take in: It's not always about you, so try not to take it personally if your partner isn't into public displays of affection. Some people simply don't feel as comfortable with physical touch as other people do.

www.ingramcontent.com/pod-product-compliance
Lightning Source LLC
LaVergne TN
LVHW020533160826
845677LV00015B/4028
9798359086981